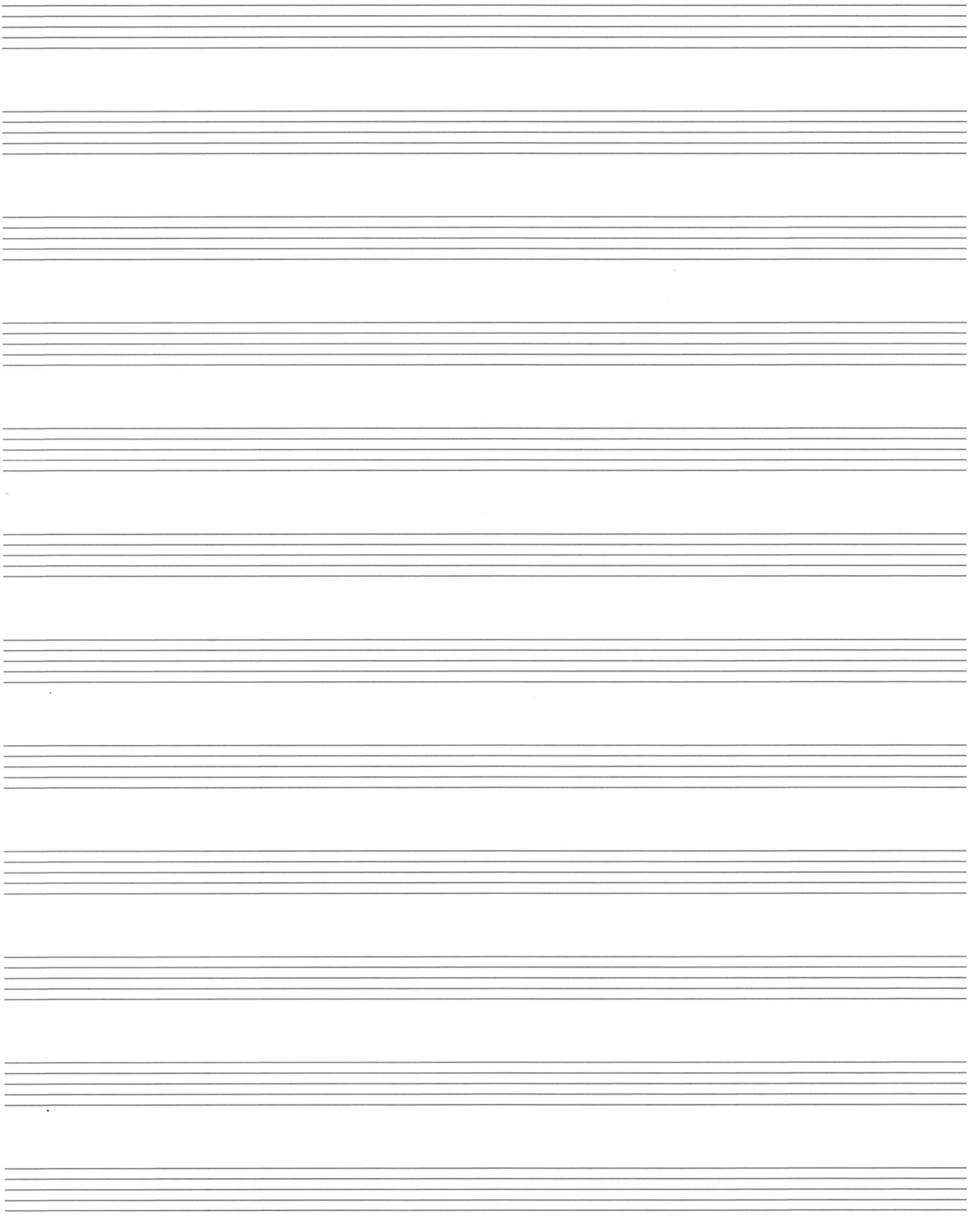

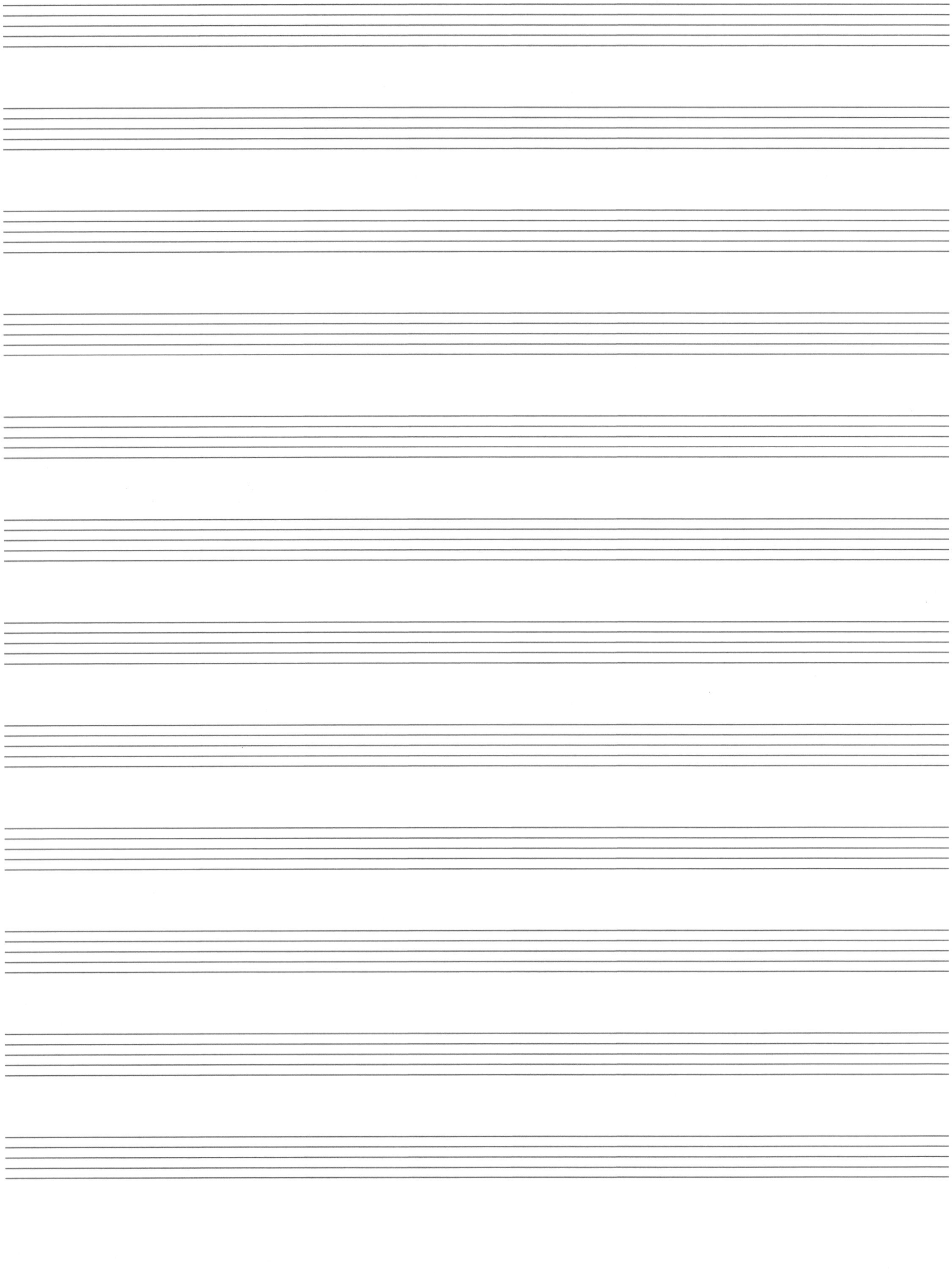

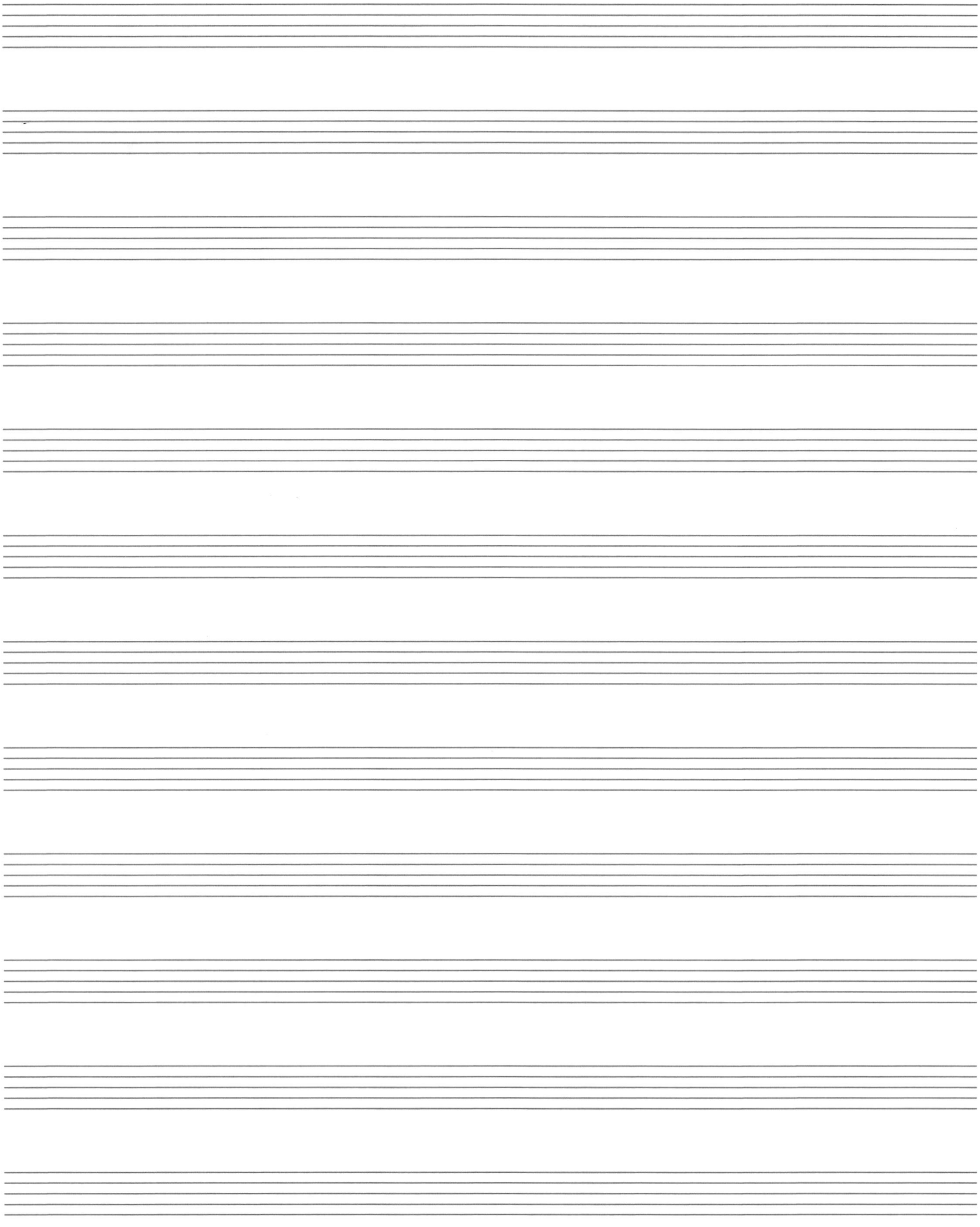

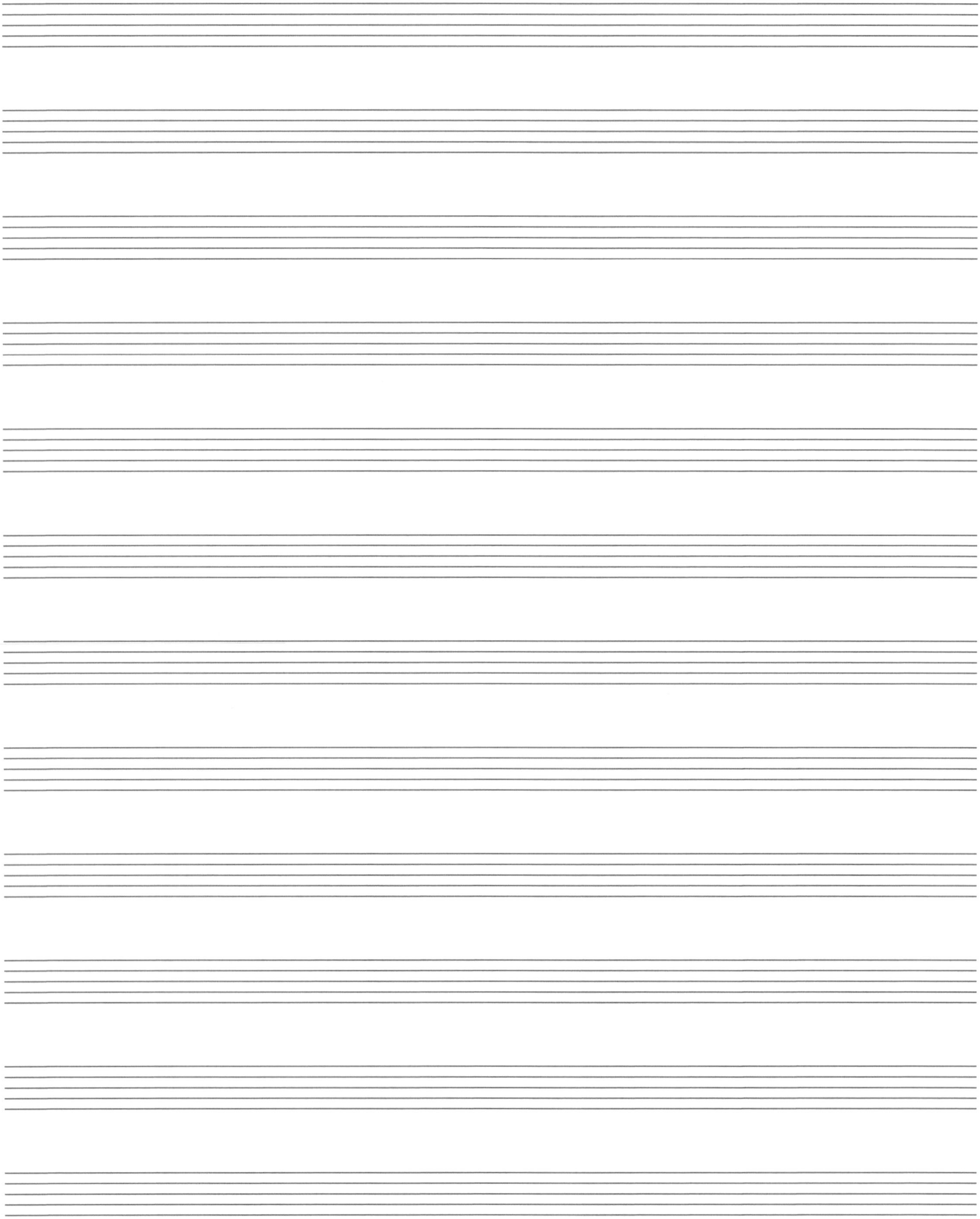

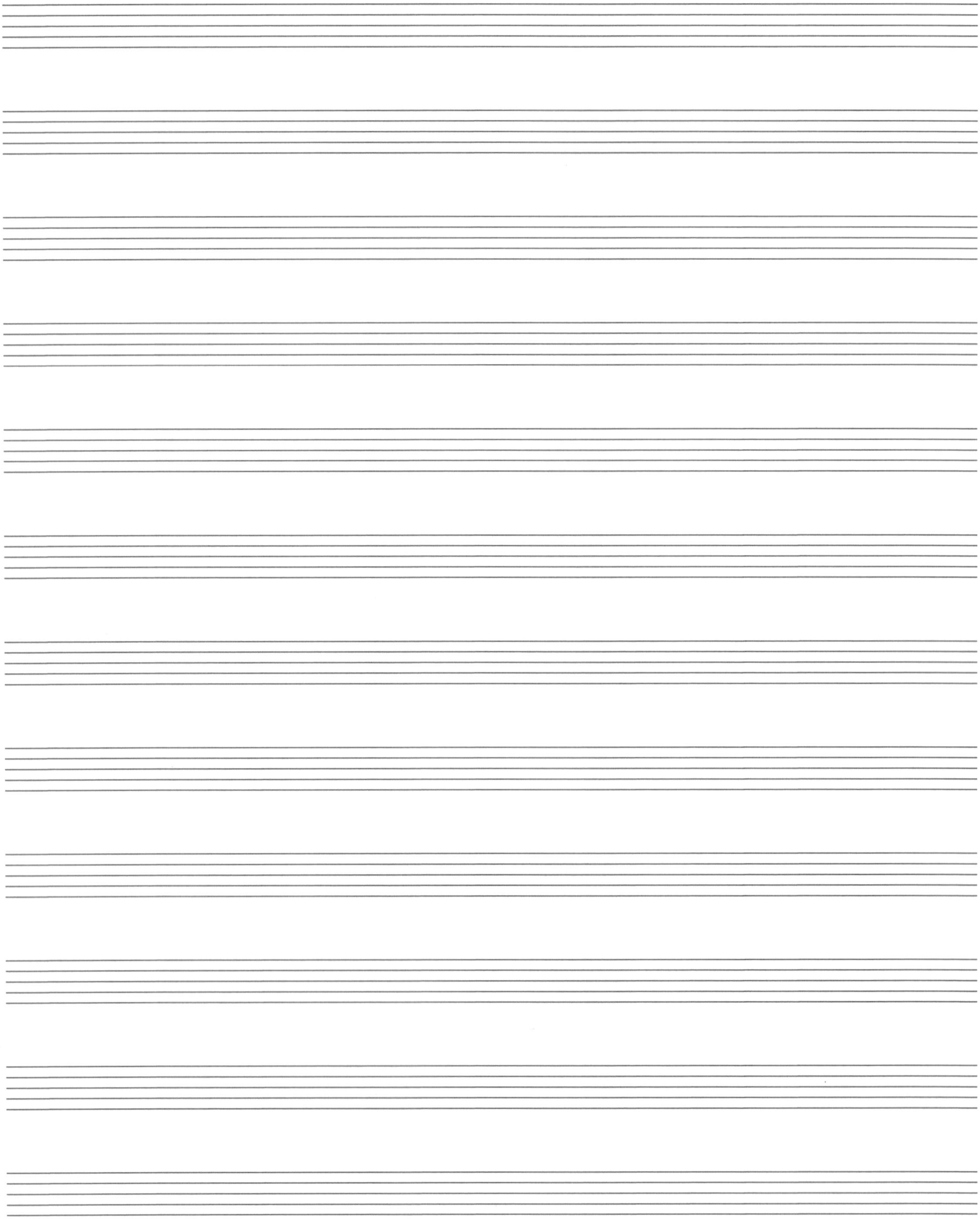

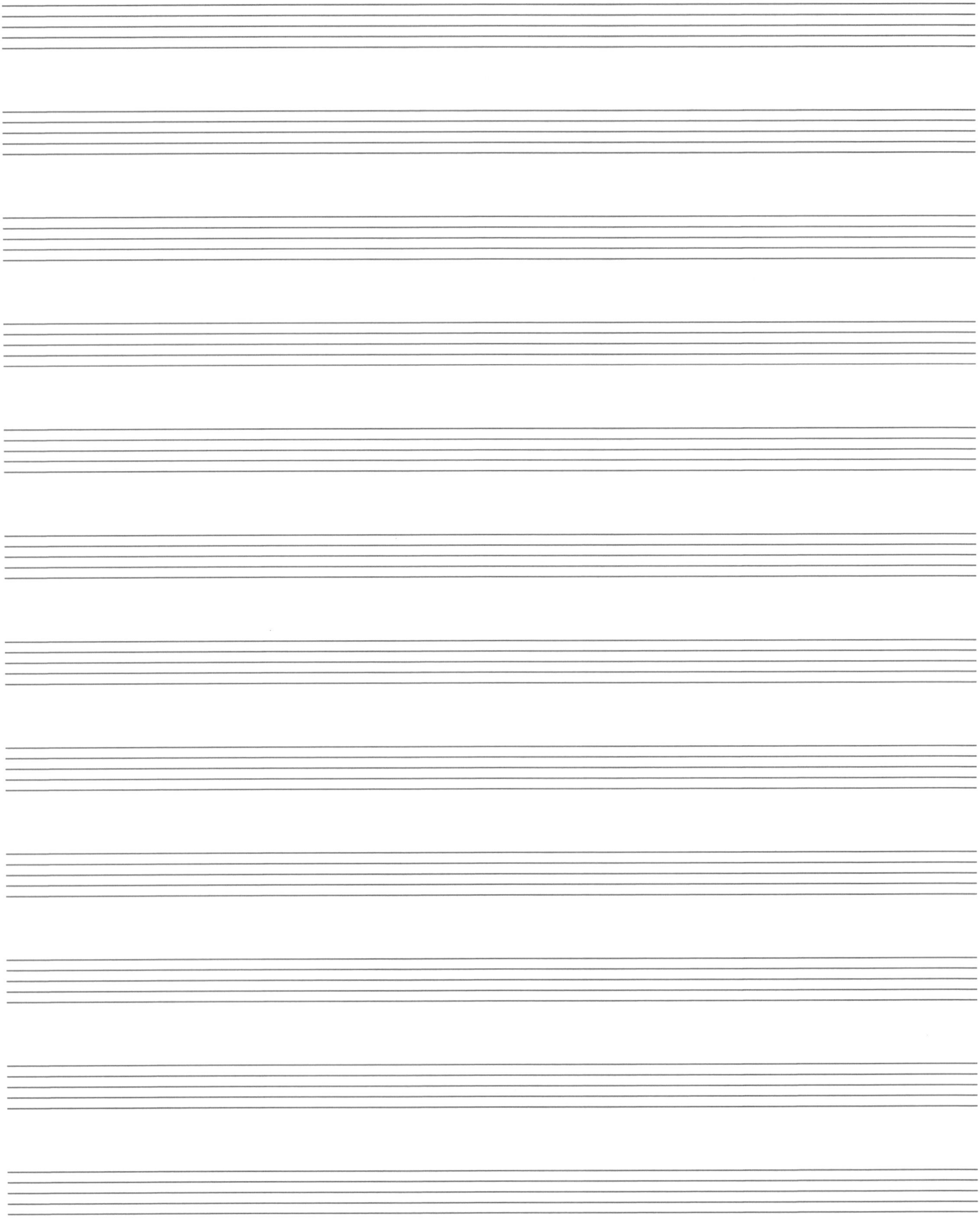

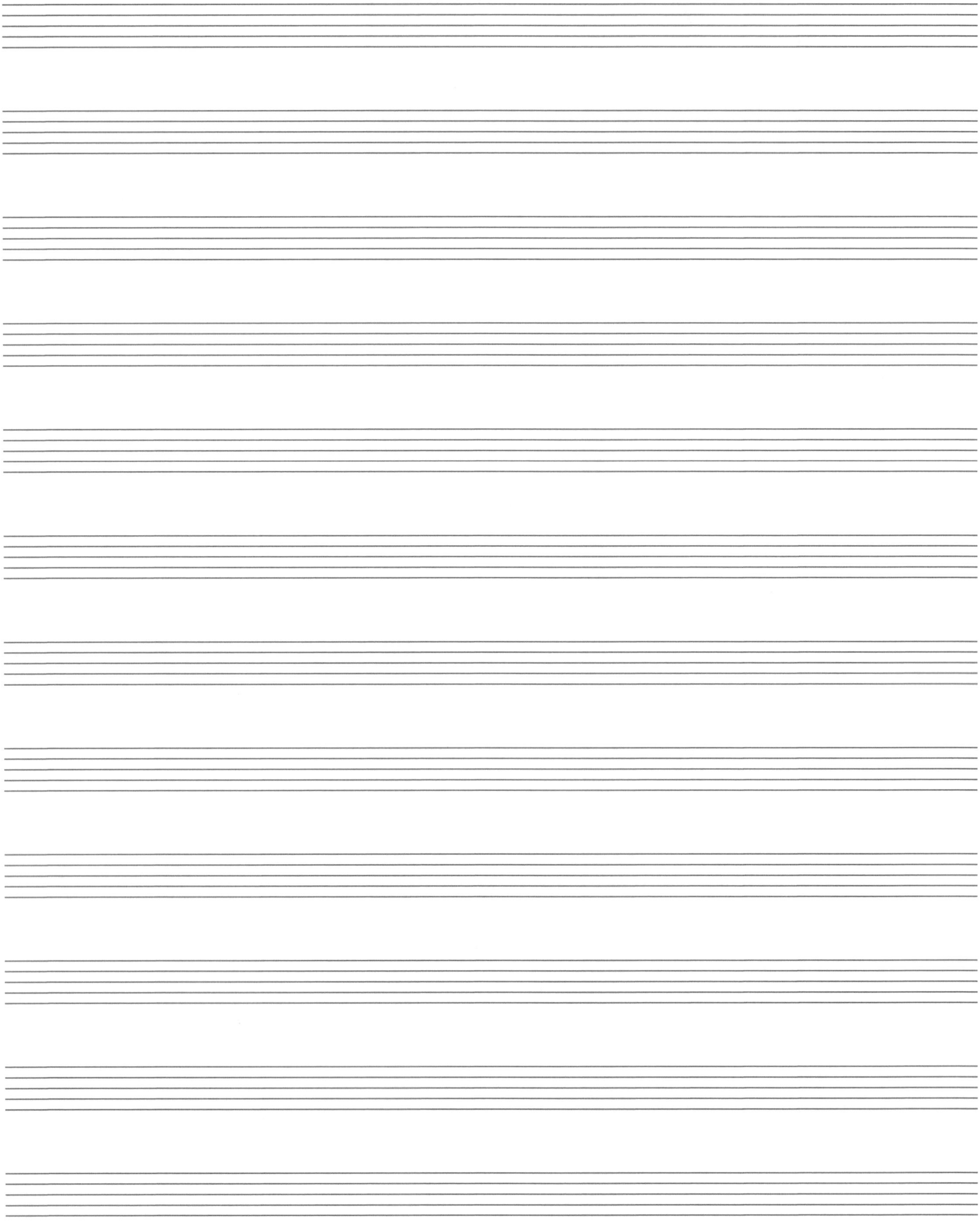

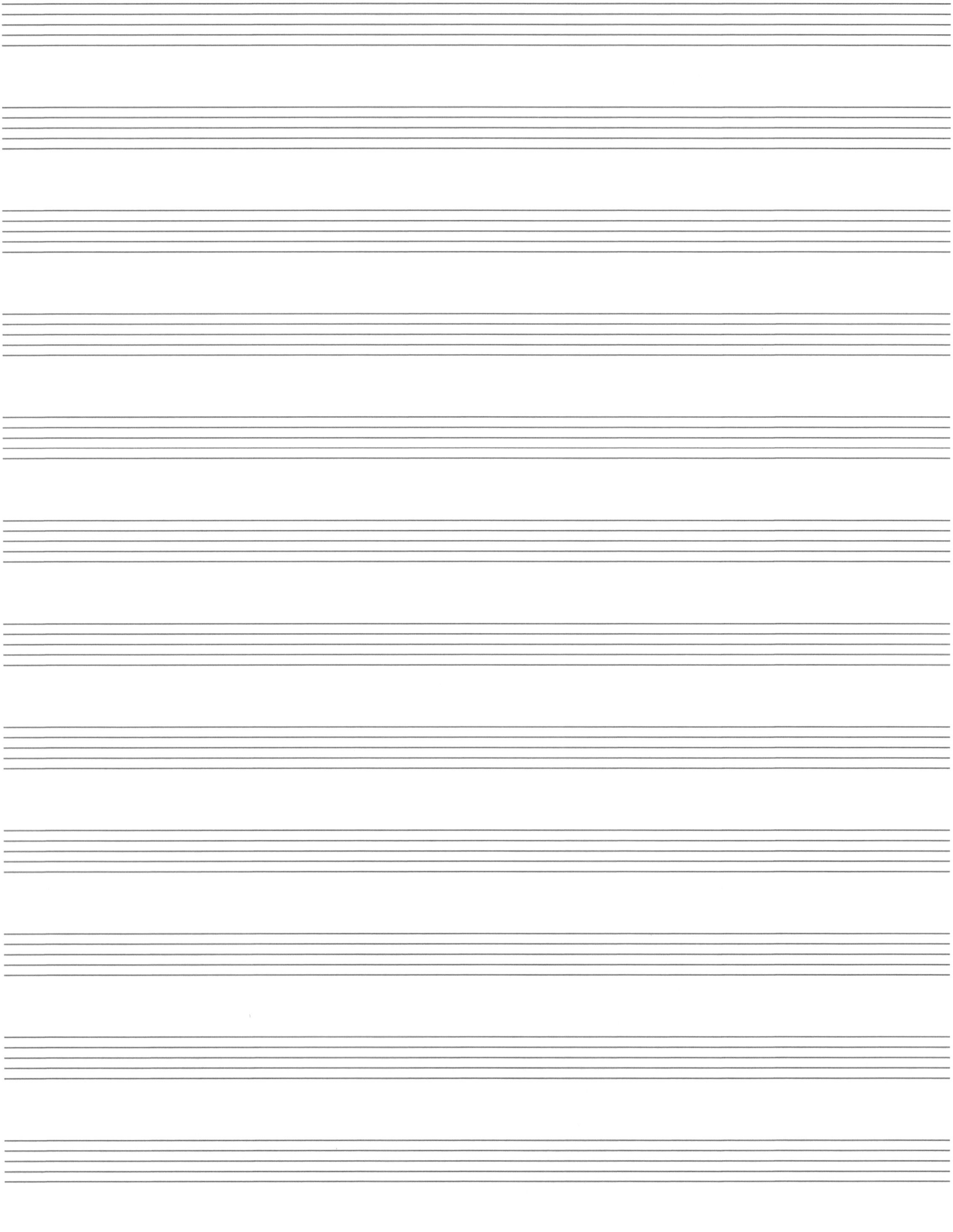

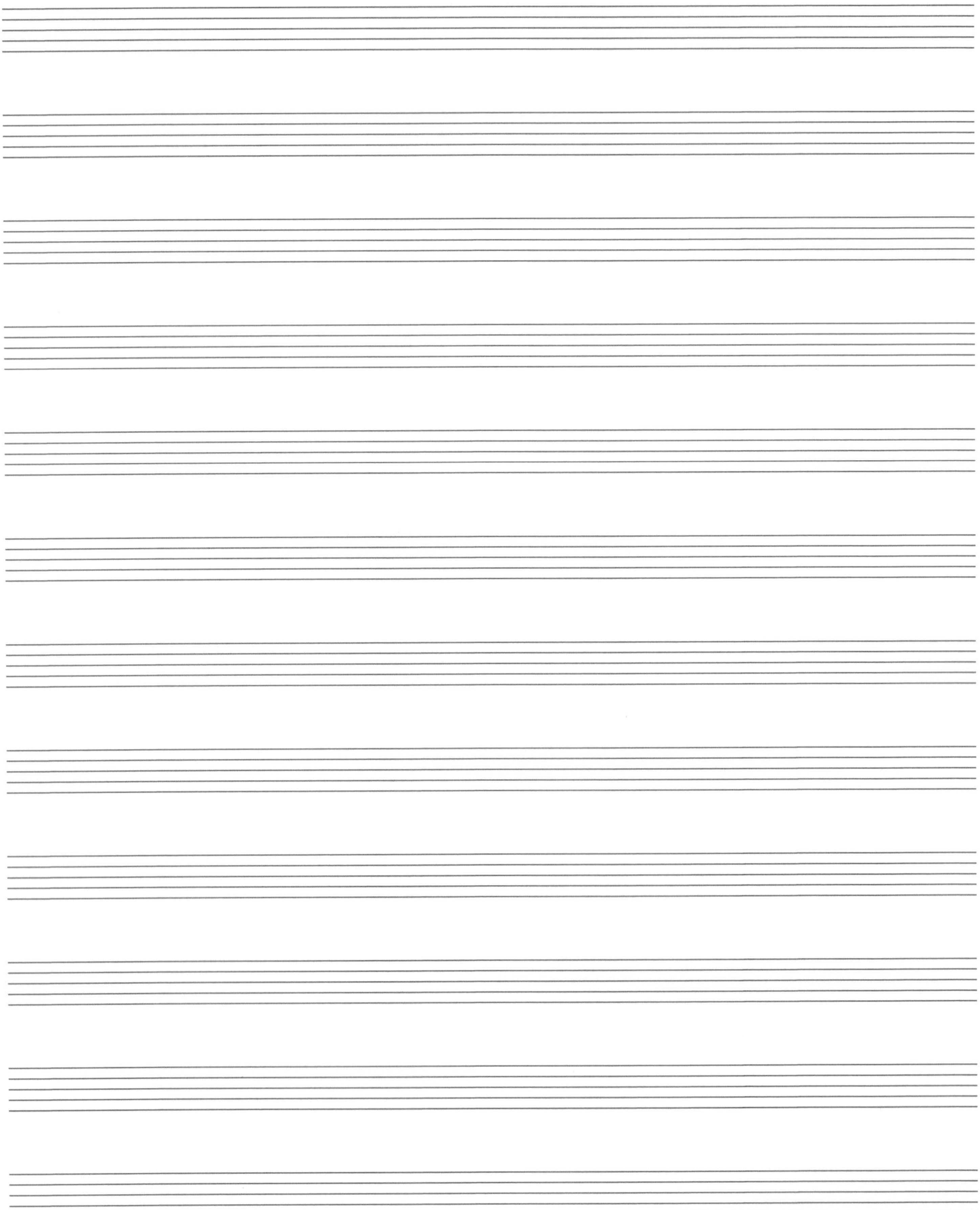

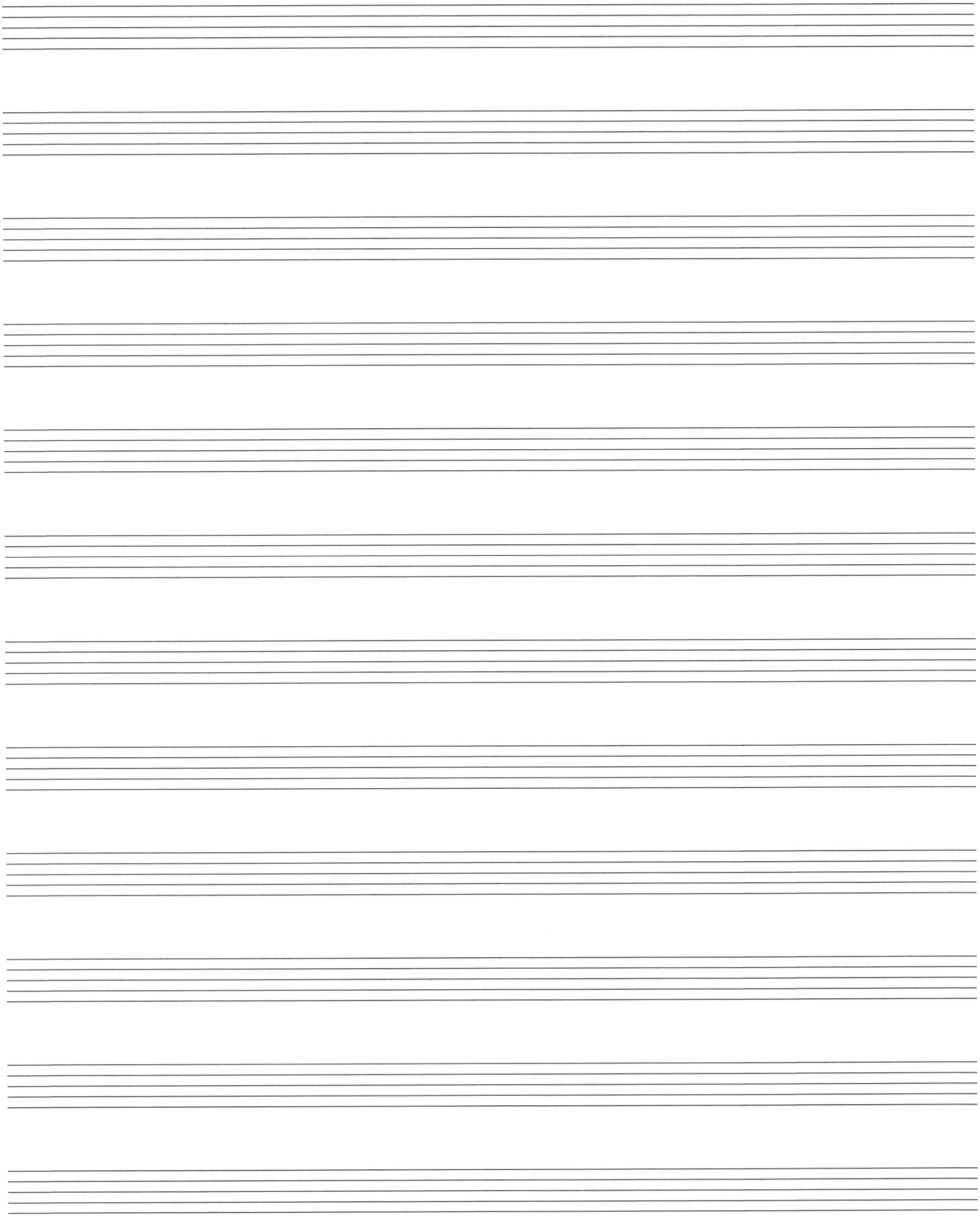

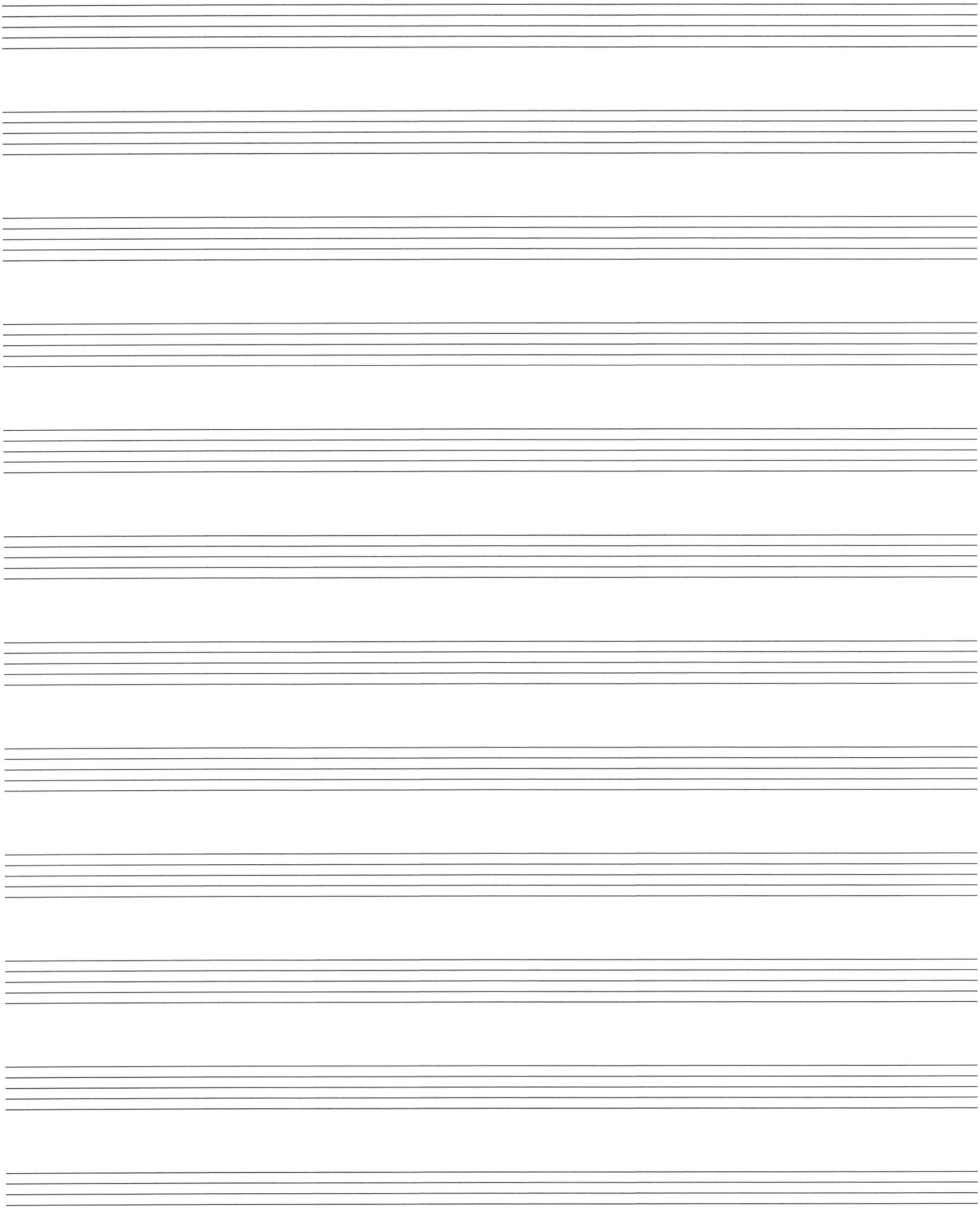

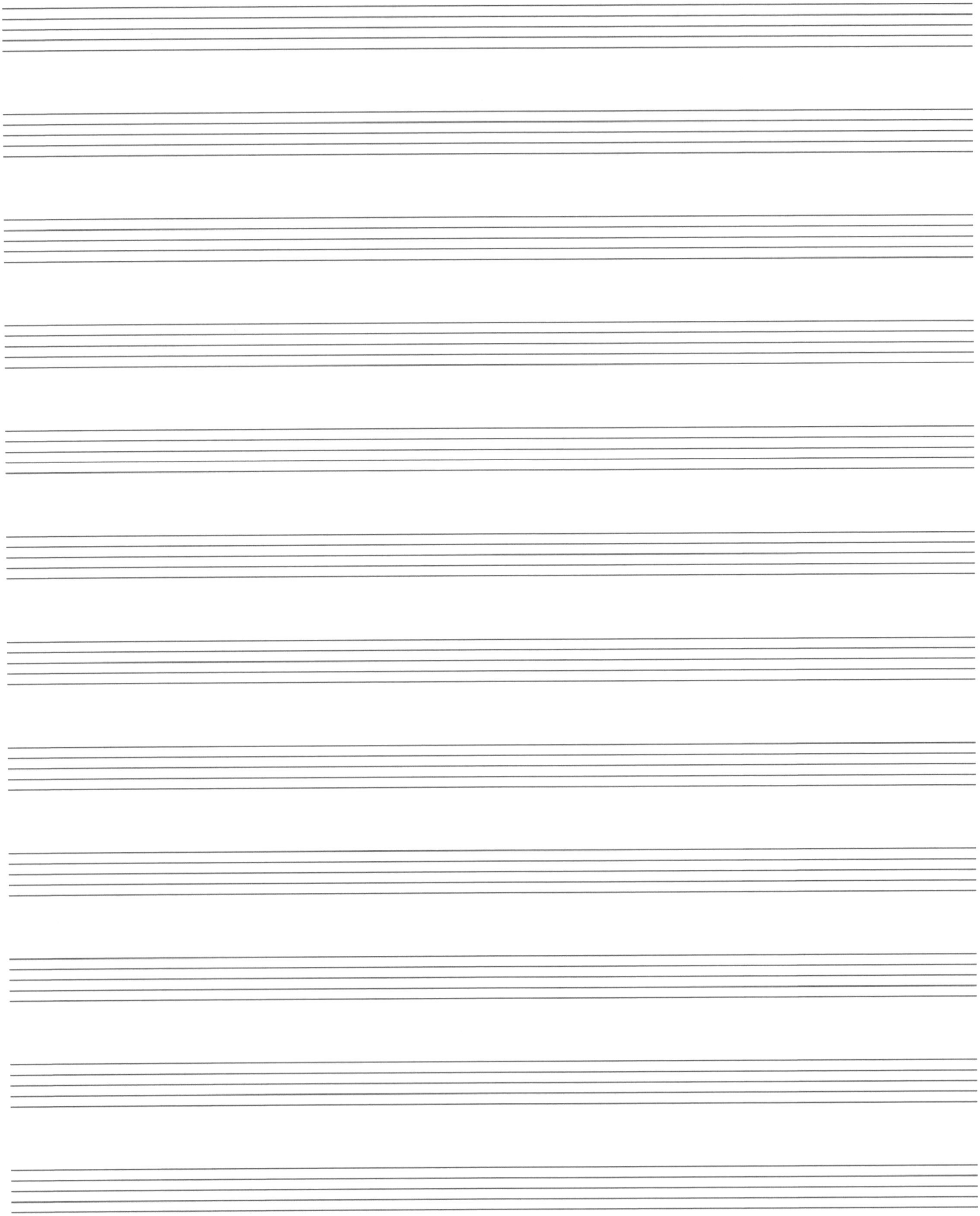

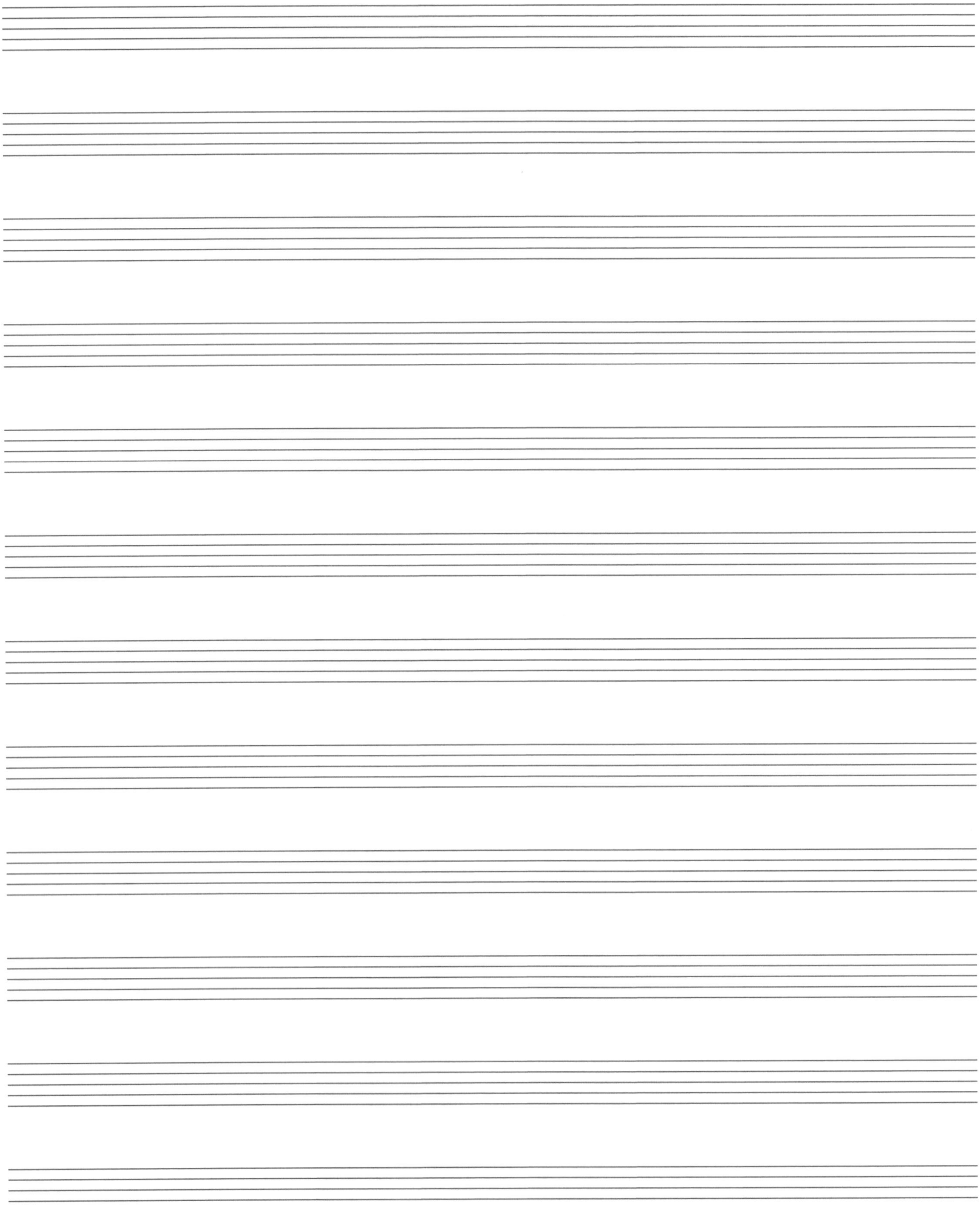

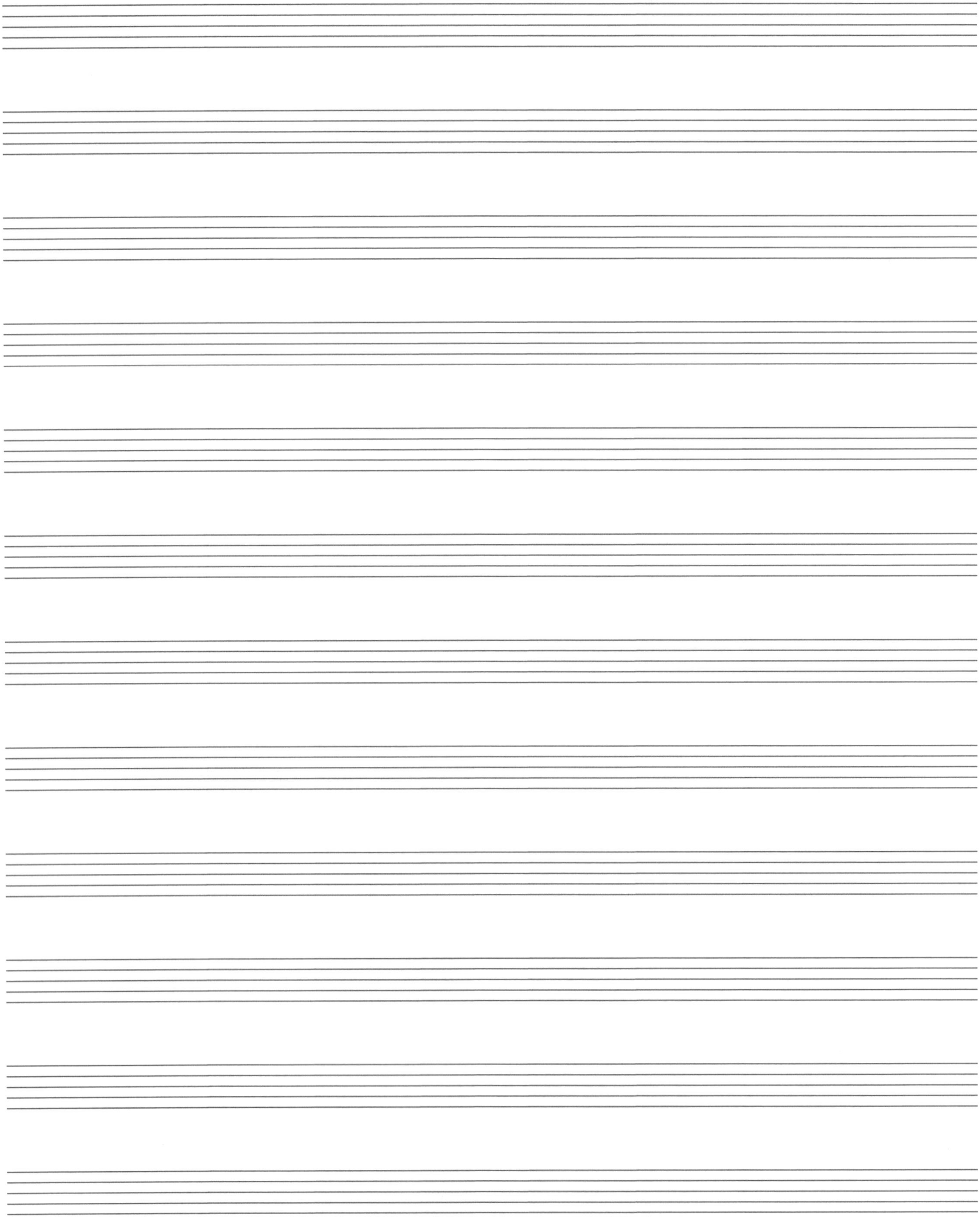

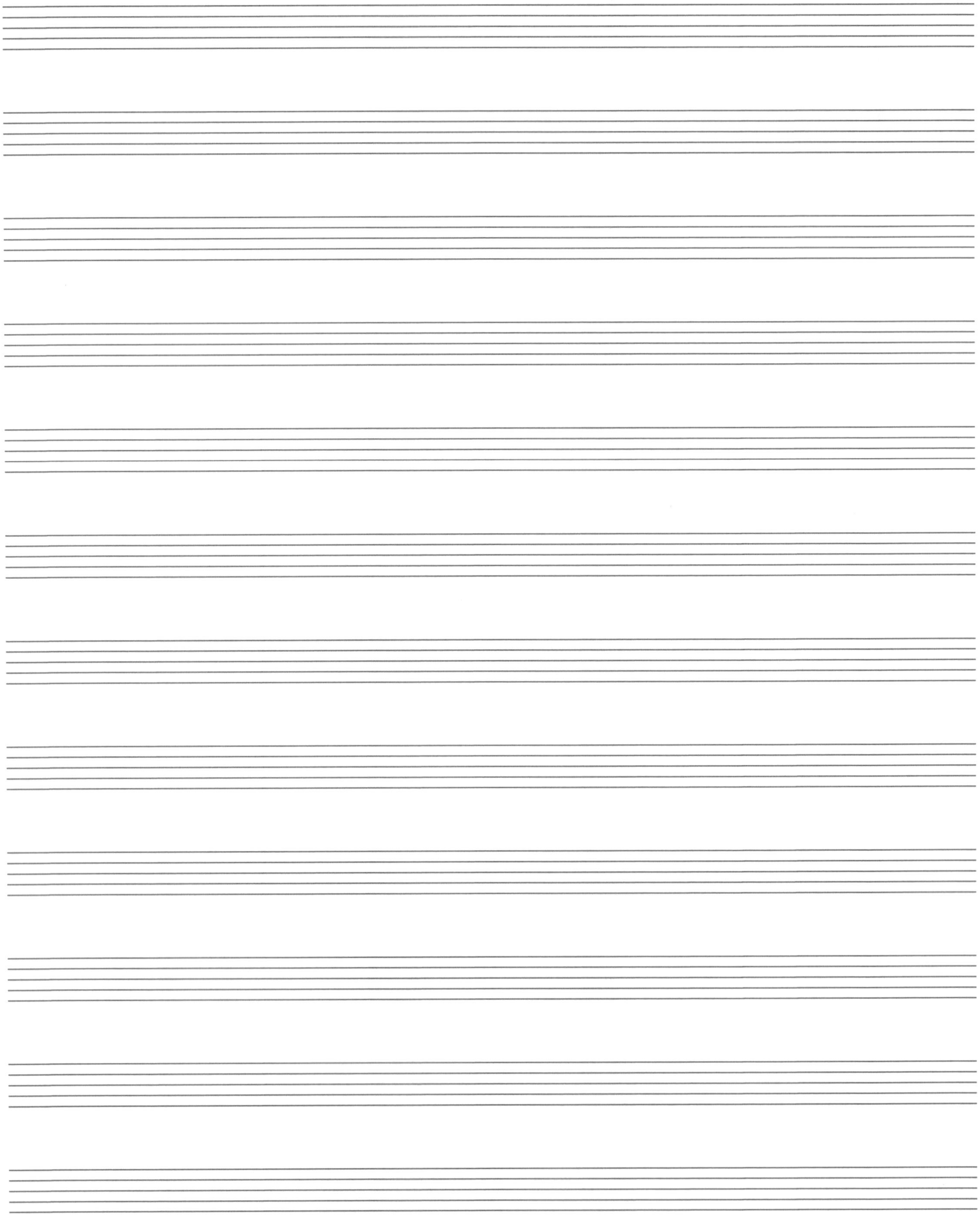

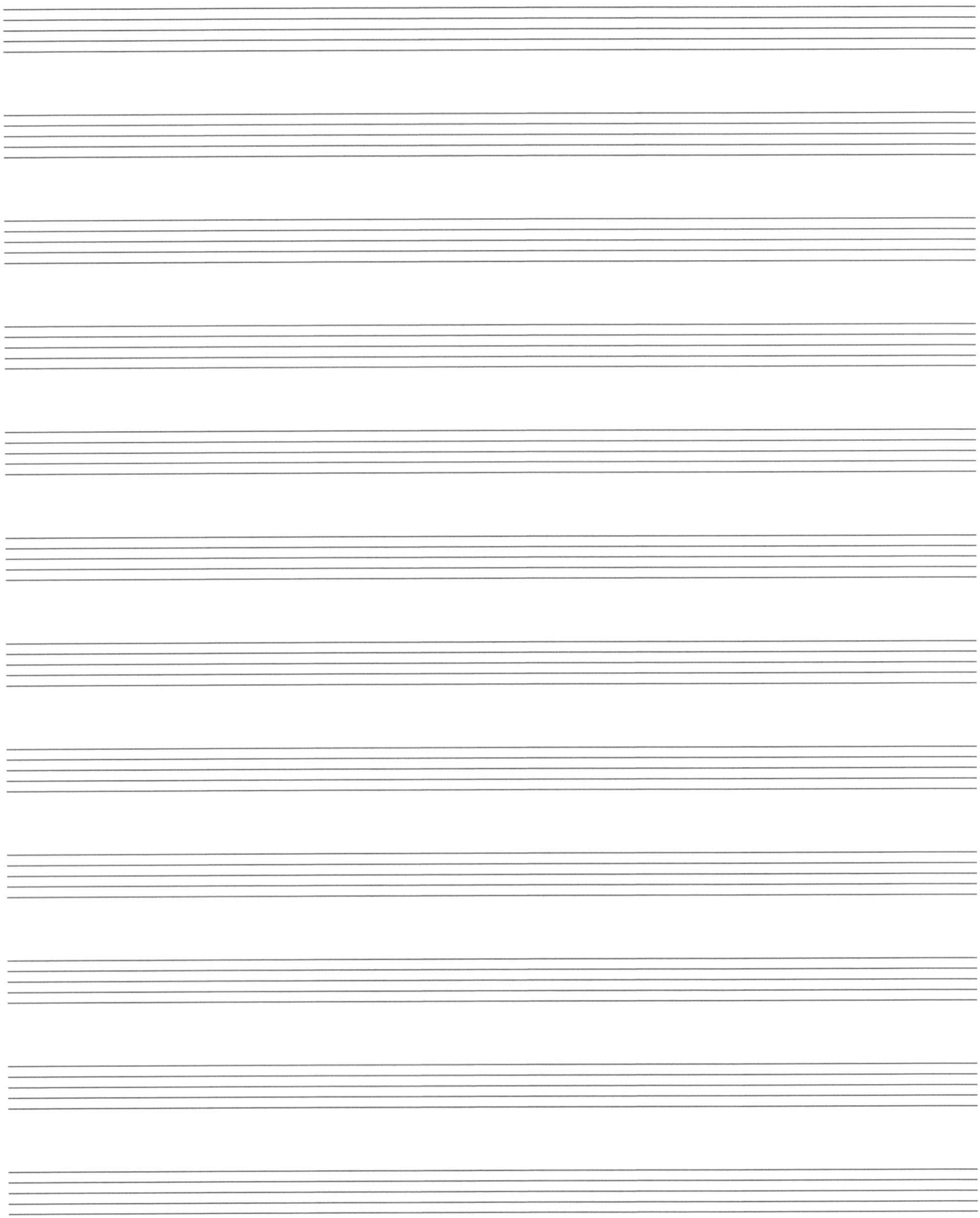

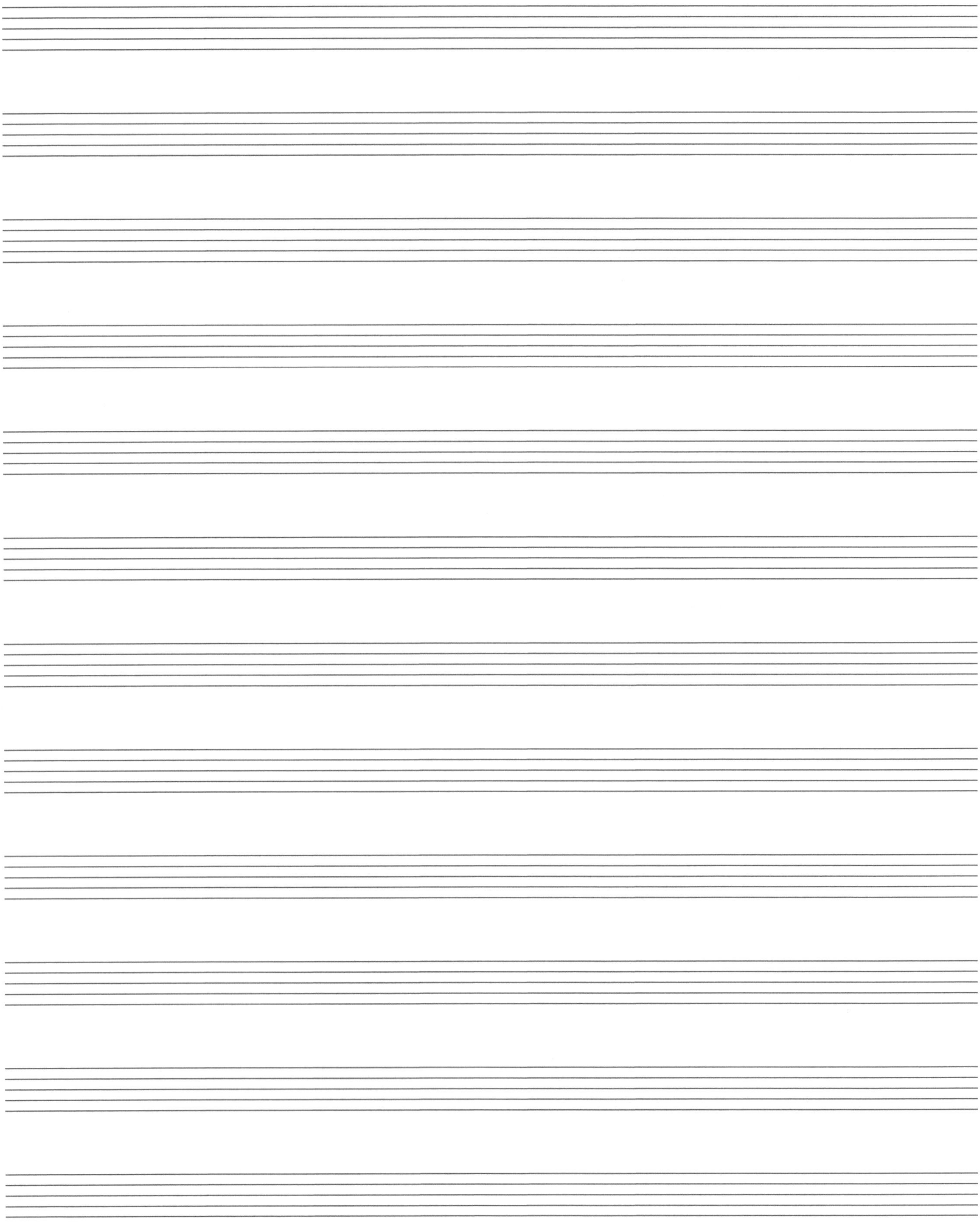

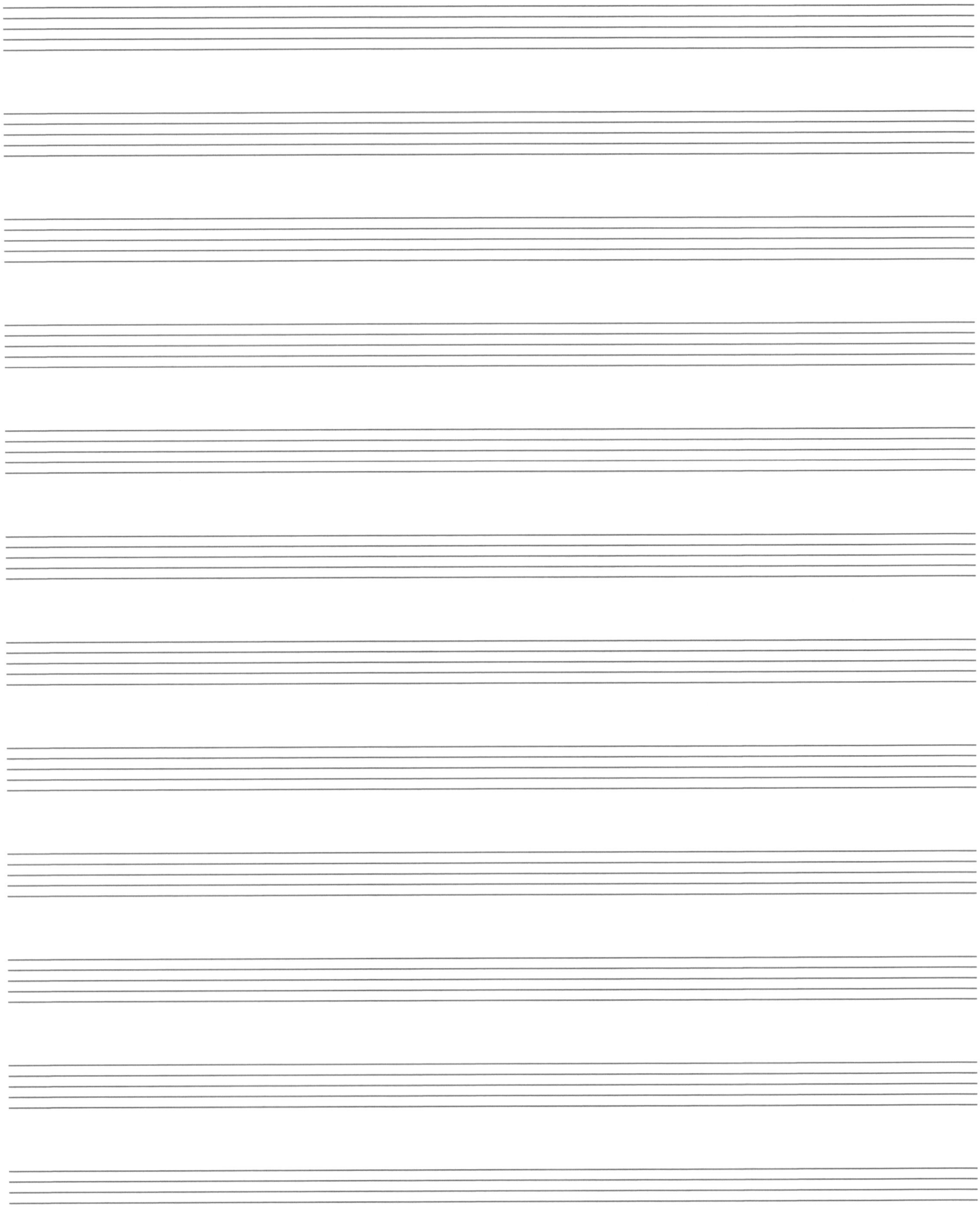

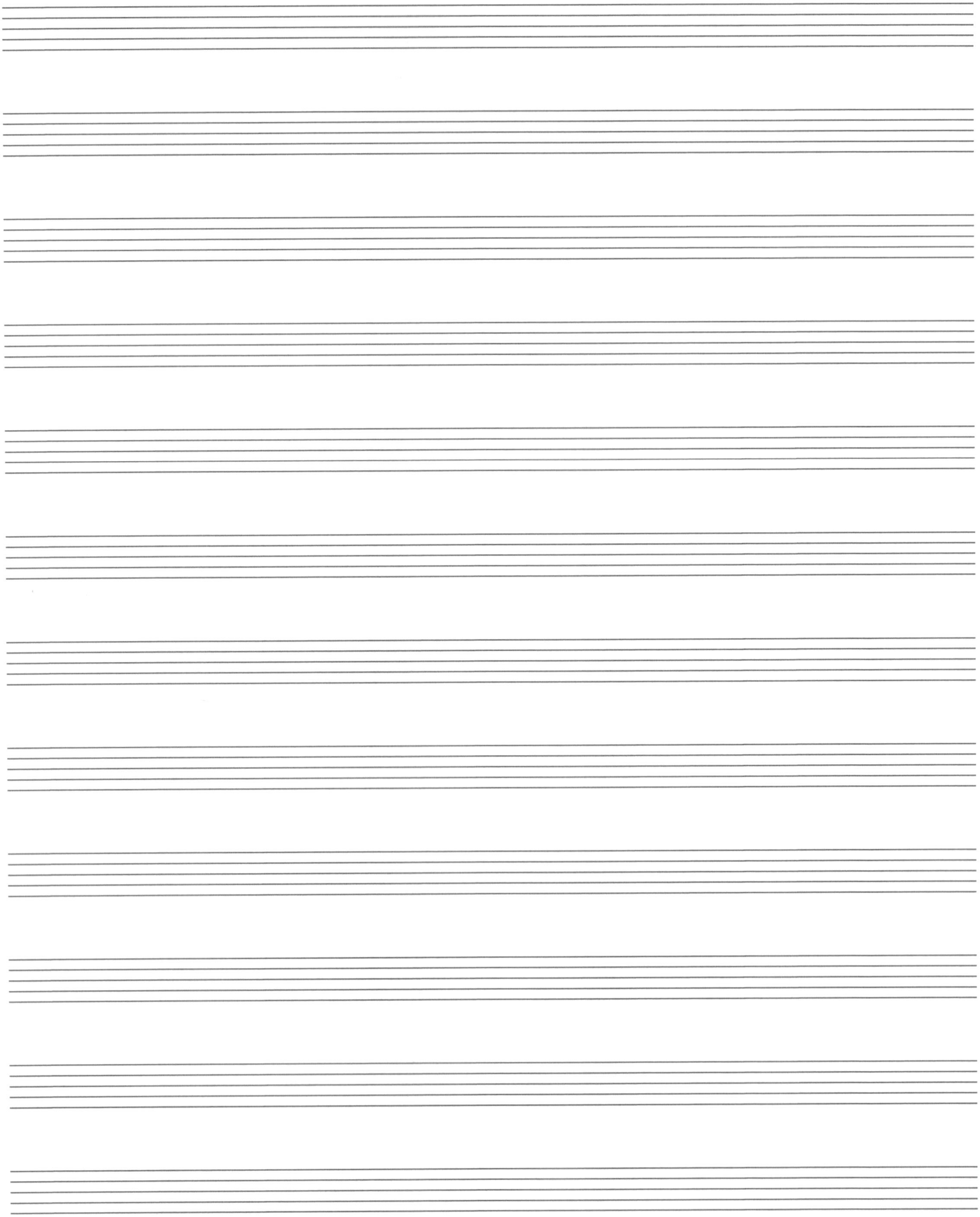

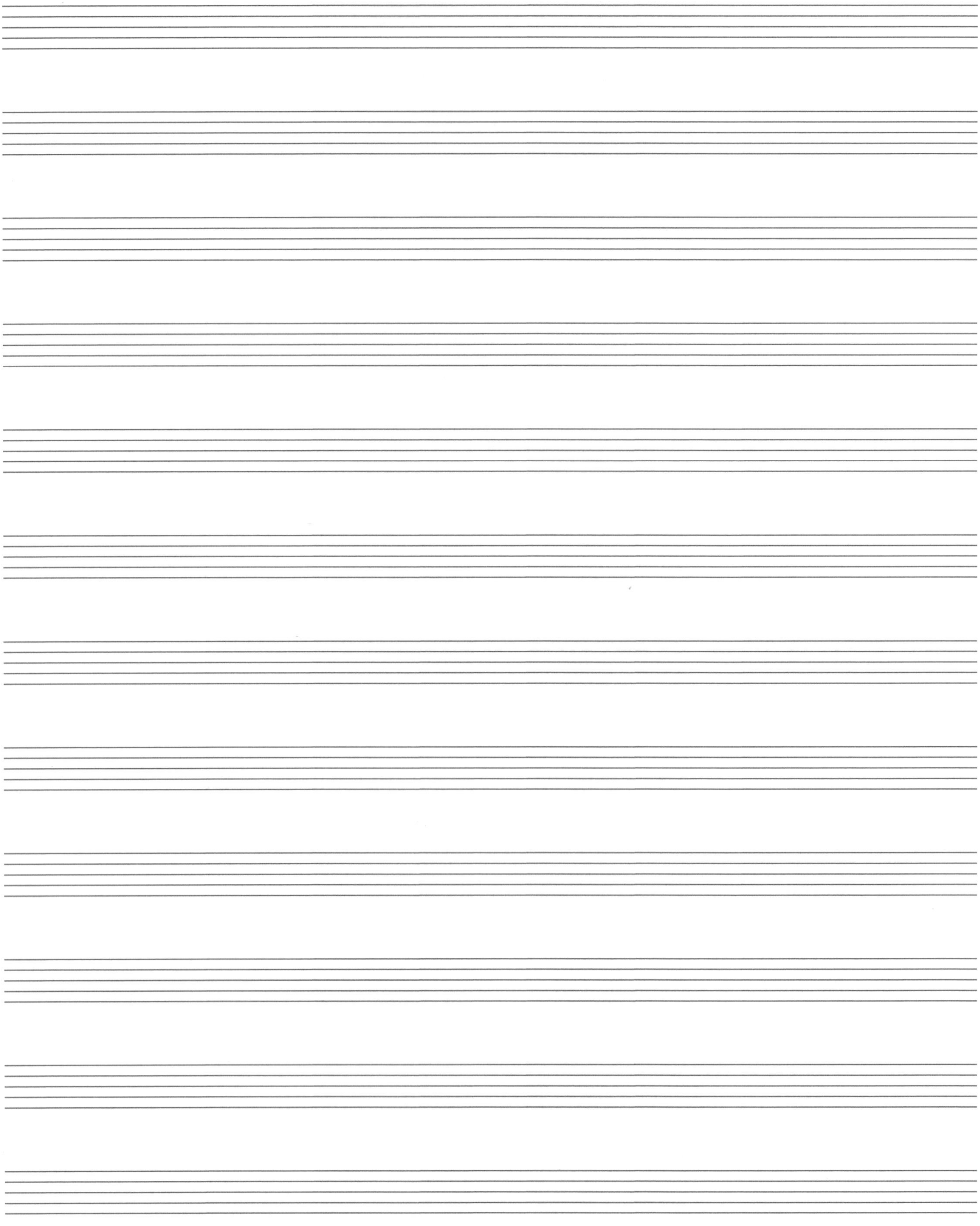

Made in United States
Troutdale, OR
12/14/2023

15870493R00073